D.W.B. Somerset
9th Feb 1990

FREEDOM, AUTHORITY
&
SCRIPTURE

D1396203

FREEDOM, AUTHORITY
&
SCRIPTURE

J. I. Packer

Foreword by Charles W. Colson

Inter-Varsity Press

Inter-Varsity Press
38 De Montfort Street, Leicester LE1 7GP, England

© Copyright 1981 by the
International Council on Biblical Inerrancy

All rights reserved. No part of this publication may be reproduced,
stored in a retrieval system, or transmitted, in any form or by any
means, electronic, mechanical, photocopying, recording or otherwise,
without the prior permission of Inter-Varsity Press.

Quotations from the Bible are from the New International Version,
© 1978 by the New York International Bible Society, published in
Great Britain by Hodder and Stoughton Ltd.

First published in the USA under the title
Freedom and Authority

First British edition 1982

British Library Cataloguing in Publication Data

Packer, J. I.
Freedom, authority and Scripture
1. Bible – evidences, authority, etc.
I. Title
220.1'3   BS480

ISBN 0–85110–445–2

Phototypeset in 11/12 Baskerville by
Nuprint Services Ltd, Harpenden, Herts.
Printed in Great Britain by Richard Clay (The Chaucer Press) Ltd.,
Bungay, Suffolk

The International Council on Biblical Inerrancy is a California-based
organization founded in 1977. It has as its purpose the defence and
application of the doctrine of biblical inerrancy as an essential element
for the authority of Scripture and a necessity for the health of the
church. It was created to counter the drift from this important
doctrinal foundation by significant segments of evangelicalism and the
outright denial of it by other church movements.

Inter-Varsity Press is the publishing division of the Universities and Colleges
Christian Fellowship (formerly the Inter-Varsity Fellowship), a student movement
linking Christian Unions in universities and colleges throughout the British Isles,
and a member movement of the International Fellowship of Evangelical Students.
For information about local and national activities in Great Britain write to
UCCF, 38 De Montfort Street, Leicester LE1 7GP.

CONTENTS

FOREWORD

A couple of years ago I was asked to speak to the International Council on Biblical Inerrancy. Believing I was too new a Christian (my conversion was in 1973), I declined. What's more, I had no experience with theological debates. My ministry was to preach the gospel and build Christian fellowships behind prison walls. 'Leave topics like inerrancy to the theologians,' I remember thinking. 'It need not concern me.'

How wrong I was! Experiences in the past two years have profoundly altered my thinking. The authority and truth of Scripture are not an obscure issue reserved for the private debate and entertainment of theologians; it is relevant, indeed critical, for every serious Christian – layman, pastor and theologian alike.

My convictions have come, not from studies in Ivory Tower academia, but from life in what may be termed the front-line trenches, behind prison walls where Christians grapple in hand-to-hand combat with the prince of darkness. In our prison fellowships, where the Bible is proclaimed as God's holy and inerrant revelation, believers grow and discipleship deepens. Christians *live* their faith with power. Where the Bible is not so proclaimed (or where Christianity is presumed to rest on subjective experience alone or content-less fellowship) faith withers and dies. Christianity without biblical fidelity is merely another passing fad in an age of passing fads. In my opinion, the issue is that clear-cut.

I've seen the same phenomena in our churches. Easy believism or 'cheap grace', as the German martyr, Dietrich Bonhoeffer, labelled it a generation ago, is rampant. It and other contemporary heresies – like 'Give to God and he'll return your gift tenfold' or 'Become a Christian and God will give you perfect bliss and heal your ingrown toenails' – are the result of trying to make Christianity appealing to a materialistic, self-centred culture on its own terms. They are also the direct result of failing to proclaim the truth of biblical revelation and accept its authority.

What we are witnessing is, in my opinion, precisely what the apostle Paul warned Timothy against: 'For the time will come when men will not put up with sound doctrine. Instead, to suit their own desires, they will gather around them a great number of teachers to say what their itching ears want to hear. They will turn their ears away from the truth and turn aside to myths' (2 Tim. 4:3, 4).

It is a bewildering paradox that one third of all American adults claim to be born-again and yet fail to make an impact on our society, which becomes sicker and more corrupt by the day. Religion is up but morality is down. The truth is that the church fails to impact the culture when the church fails to stand and act on biblical truth. Sadly, we have become like the world, instead of standing against it in 'a majestic witness to the holy commandments of God', as Carl Henry put it so well.

Inerrancy, then, is no theoretical question. It is crucial to the church's role in the world. It reveals whether God's power is to be exercised through us, whether we are indeed God's holy nation, or just another 'how-to-find-yourself' cult.

So read on and prepare yourself. May this book help and equip you to do as Paul, in answer to the danger of false teaching, commanded Timothy to do: 'Preach the Word; be prepared in season and out of season; correct, rebuke and encourage – with great patience and careful instruction' (2 Tim. 4:2).

Charles W. Colson

PREFACE
TO THE BRITISH EDITION

The following essay was written at the request of the International Council on Biblical Inerrancy, a body of which an anonymous but clearly official UCCF author said in the June 1980 edition of the *Christian Graduate*: 'ICBI has done a useful and constructive job. We can be grateful to them for their stand. They are not an extreme fundamentalist group and, contrary to the fears of some observers, their statements are balanced, scholarly and well based on Scripture. We would want to associate ourselves with them in their position.' For these words I, as a spiritual child of UCCF and also an ICBI member, was, I hope, properly grateful.

Charles Colson's Foreword crystallizes the sense of things I have sought to express in the essay. Too often the doctrine of Scripture is treated as an essentially academic question. This is because professional scholars take the lead in discussing it, and regularly arrange the discussion round specific 'critical' problems thrown up in their teaching. But the question is in fact practical. It is really about knowing, trusting, obeying and proving God as a way of life. It is an illusion to think that differences of opinion about the meaning and trustworthiness of the various strands of biblical instruction make no difference to one's thoughts about God, one's relationship to him, and one's moral practice. What is actually at stake is whether, or how far, we learn the secret of supernatural living and of pleasing God. No doubt some are better at this point than their professed beliefs give them any right to be, just as some whose beliefs seem correct fail to live consistently by what they know. Granting this, however, we must still face the fact that to approach Scripture as God's authentic and infallible utterance, to put full trust in the Christ and the promises which Scripture presents, and to revere biblical moral teaching as God's orders to his children, is the entry into a life of joy and power which those who decline this approach, whether they call themselves Christians and maintain devotional routines or not, are going to miss.

My essay is a heart-cry in a catastrophic age about the difference it makes to personal and community life when our relation to the Bible and its Christ is as it should be. Whether you see its theme as the Bible's transforming power or the remaking of mankind will depend on what you bring to the reading of it – where you are coming from, as Americans say; and either way, I shall not mind. If I can convince you of the connection between these two things, my object will be achieved.

J. I. Packer

1

AUTHORITY
AND FREEDOM

'Authority' is a word that makes most people think of law and order, direction and restraint, command and control, dominance and submission, respect and obedience. How, I wonder, do you react to such ideas? Have they any place in your vision of the life that is good and sweet? If so, you are unusual. One tragedy of our time is that, having these associations, 'authority' has become almost a dirty word in the Western world, while opposition to authority in schools, families and society generally is cheerfully accepted as something that is at least harmless and perhaps rather fine.

How is it that so many today will tolerate expressions of defiance and disorder in society which a century ago would have been thought intolerable? Whence came the passionate permissiveness that has made a shambles of so many homes, schools and individual lives? What goes on here? What is happening to us?

The quest for freedom
The answer to these questions is pinpointed by the fact that 'freedom' is today almost a magic word.

Since World War 2, when those who fought the dictators defined their war aims in terms of Four Freedoms – freedom from want, freedom from fear, freedom of speech and freedom of religion – freedom in one form or another has been a worldwide passion, encouraged and catered to at every level. Therapists labour to induce freedom from inhibitions. *Playboy* carries the torch for sexual freedom ('free love' as it was once called, though there is little enough real love in *Playboy* sex). Campaigning politicians promise freedom from this or that social evil. Young nations seek freedom from the domination of overbearing neighbours. Artists pursue freedom from conventions of form and style which bound their predecessors.

Longings for freedom from restrictions, from the dead hand of the past, from disliked pressures, obligations, systems and what not are for many people the strongest of life's driving forces. Freedom – 'getting out from under' as we say – has become modern man's obsession. And freedom is always seen as involving rejection of authority! Authority is equated with fixed limits, freedom with cutting loose from all that. Hence the crisis of authority which marks our time.

This way of conceiving freedom has its roots in philosophy: in dreams of the perfectibility of man, in Rousseau's idea that civilization squeezes you out of shape, in the educationists' fancy that inside each little demon is a little angel waiting to come out as soon as mechanical pressures relax and interest is wooed. It is rooted in experience too. Bad experiences of harsh and stifling authority at home,

14

at school, in church, with the boss or the police, or elsewhere in the body politic, have fuelled fires of revolt. Who can wonder when rebels are hostile to what hurt them? The effect is that all forms of authority are seen as cell walls, which makes the quest for freedom feel like a Great Escape from some ideological prison-camp. Undisguised contempt for restrictions and directions, and truculent defiance which bucks all systems when it is not busy exploiting them, have become almost conventional, and anyone who respects authority stands out as odd. Modern man may claim to have come of age, but from this standpoint he seems to have regressed to adolescence. (Adolescents, of course, are always first to insist on their own adulthood.) Surely today's rebellion against authority is a sign not of maturity but of its opposite. It is a form of folly, not of wisdom. It leads only to decadence and spoilt lives.

The truth, paradoxical yet inescapable, is this: there is no freedom apart from external authority. To say 'I am my own authority, a law to myself' is to enslave myself to myself, which, as Seneca (the Roman moralist) said, is the worst bondage of all. Only as I bow to an authority which is not myself am I ever free. Let me explain.

What is authority?
Authority is a relational word which signifies the right to rule. It is expressed in claims and is acknowledged by compliance and conformity. The word is used abstractly for the commanding quality which authoritative claims have, and also concretely for the source of such claims – 'the authority' in

each case. There are various sorts and sources of authority. Documents and authors are 'the authorities' for scholars, statutes and past decisions for lawyers, parents for their young children, governors and law enforcement personnel for us all. In the realms of belief, truth has authority; in realms of behaviour, authority belongs to the moral law.

When historic Christianity receives the Bible as an absolute authority for creed and conduct, it does so on the basis that since God is a God of truth and righteousness, that which he lays before us in writing must have the same qualities. The current inerrancy debate about whether we should treat all Bible teaching as true and right is really about how far we can regard Scripture as authoritative.

Exercise of authority in its various spheres is not necessarily *authoritarian*. There is a crucial distinction here. Authoritarianism is authority corrupted, gone to seed. Authoritarianism appears when the submission that is demanded cannot be justified in terms of truth or morality. Nazism, Communism and Jim Jones's cult in Guyana are examples. Any form of human authority can degenerate in this way. You have authoritarianism in the state when the regime uses power in an unprincipled way to maintain itself. You have it in churches when leaders claim control of their followers' consciences. You have it in academic work at school, university or seminary when you are required to agree with your teacher rather than follow the evidence of truth for yourself. You have it in the family when parents direct or restrict their children unreasonably. Unhappy experiences of authority are usually experiences of degenerate authority, that is, of authoritarianism. That such experiences leave a bad taste and prompt scepticism about authority in all its forms is sad but not surprising.

Authoritarianism is evil, anti-social, anti-human and ultimately anti-God (for self-deifying pride is at its heart), and I have nothing to say in its favour. Legal and executive power may be present to enforce authoritarian demands, but nothing can make them respectable or praiseworthy. Even when unprincipled requirements have legal right on their side, as they sometimes do, they remain demands which it was morally wrong to make.

When Christians affirm the authority of the Bible, meaning that biblical teaching reveals God's will and is the instrument of his rule over our lives, part of what they are claiming is that Scripture sets before us the factual and moral nature of things. God's law corresponds to created human nature, so that in fulfilling his requirements we fulfil ourselves, and the gospel of Christ answers to actual human need as glove fits hand, so that all our responses to God make for our good and no touch of authoritarianism enters into his exercise of authority over us.

We talk about authority in order to sort out what factors in a situation should determine our attitudes and actions. The goal of such talk is to ensure that right decisions, properly reached, do in fact get made. Whenever we credit something with authority – a textbook, a ruling, a document or whatever – we mean that in its own sphere it is more or less decisive as a guide to what should be said or done. When the risen Christ told his disciples, 'All *authority* in heaven and on earth has been given to me' (Mt. 28:18), one implication was that all people everywhere should recognize his reign and treat his words as having decisive force for their lives. So he continued, 'Therefore go and make disciples of all nations . . . teaching them to obey everything I have commanded you' (verses. 19, 20). When Christians debate whether Christ's authority attaches to what the church teaches or to what individual Christians think or to what the Bible says, they are not suggesting that these three never coincide or that two of them have no authority at all. What they are trying to decide is which of the three is *decisive*. The giving of decisive direction is what authority is all about.

Authority in human lives

Clearly, then, authority-principles will have formative and integrative effects on the communities and individuals that embrace them. By imposing a consistent method of decision-making, they dispel haphazardness and to that extent unify one's living. Those who acknowledge them as binding are left feeling that in trying to observe them you are doing what you should and that this makes life meaningful and worthwhile. To Christians, non-Christian authority-principles often seem ruinously wrong – the Marxist authority-principle, for instance, which requires everyone to work on a materialist basis for the socialized society that lies beyond the revolution, or the cultists' authority-principle that their leader (Sun Myung Moon or Jim Jones or whoever) should be listened to as God's infallible spokesman, or the authority-principle which prescribes the Buddhist,

Hindu or Islamic way of living. Yet it remains true that any fixed authority-principle gives life a goal and shape, a target, a programme and a yardstick of achievement, which it would not otherwise have. Only the Christian authority-principle leads to man's chief end (glorifying and enjoying God, as the Shorter Catechism puts it). Yet just as drugs with lethal long-term effects, like heroin and cocaine, will for the moment make you feel brighter, so any authority-principle, however dubious, will in the short term make its devotees feel brighter – more integrated, more purposeful, more in shape – than they would feel with no such principle to hold their lives together. He who knows no obligation to do anything lives the saddest, most aimless, most distracted life of all.

So the anti-authority syndrome now current in the West, leading as it does to lives of haphazard hedonism in which my feelings of like and dislike are the only authority I recognize, is a major human tragedy. You could hardly get further from the way we are meant to live.

Nor is the tragedy just personal. It touches society too. History shows that many of the values basic to what we call civilization as opposed to savagery are biblical and Christian in origin. The world never knew them till it started living by the Christian authority-principle, and without that principle these values are unlikely to survive, at least in the decadent West as we know it. Take two examples.

First, we have inherited a belief in the dignity of womanhood and in the duty of men to honour and protect what Peter calls the weaker (more vulnerable, sooner hurt, thinner-skinned) sex (1 Pet. 3:7). This is founded in the scriptural teaching that both sexes bear God's image and share the same vocation as deputy governors of his world (Gn. 1:26–30), but it derives most directly, it would seem, from the unfailing courtesy, respect and goodwill towards women shown by Jesus (*cf.* Mk. 7:25ff.; 14:3ff.; Lk. 7:11ff., 36ff.; 8:43ff.; 10:38ff.; 13:10ff.; 23:27ff.; Jn. 4:7ff.; 8:2ff.; 11:20ff.; 20:11ff.; *etc.*). In the ancient Jewish and pagan world, as in Islam today, however important the woman's role as child-bearer, nurturer and homemaker, it was taken for granted that she was the male's natural inferior as a human being. By changing that, Christianity did more to raise women's status than any other movement in history. When Women's Libbers censure biblical Christians for their doubts as to whether the fulfilling by women of historic male-leadership roles in church and state is pleasing to God, they usually forget that the starting point of their own arguments, that is the equal dignity of man and woman, is itself a Christian insight which can only be expected to fade when the authority of Christian truth is denied. It will be small gain for women to have achieved professional interchangeability with men if meantime men lapse into thinking that the height of masculinity is to treat women as playthings, each one fair game for male marauders.

Scripture knows the world of lust well (*cf.* Gn. 34; 35:22; 2 Sa. 11; 13) and seeks to wean us from it (Mt. 5:27ff.; 1 Cor. 6:9f.; Gal. 5:19ff.; Col. 3:5; 1 Thes. 4:3ff.; *etc.*). But any generation that devalues Scripture may be expected to revert to that level.

Indeed, we see it happening already. The *Playboy* philosophy, with the rest of the pattern of decline which Paul luridly pictures in Romans 1:21–32, Ephesians 4:18f. and Colossians 3:5–8, is more familiar and socially acceptable today than it has been for centuries, and it looks like becoming yet more so.

Second, we have inherited a belief in the sanctity of human life. This reflects the biblical insistence that we honour God by protecting and preserving the life he gives to us his image-bearers, and that we dishonour him if we snuff that life out (save in judicial execution and war, which Scripture sees as special cases: *cf.* Gn. 9:6; Ex. 20:13 with 21:12–17; Rom. 13:4; Jos. 8:1–29; Jdg. 15:14ff.; *etc.*). Paganism, by contrast, has always held life cheap. Pagan philosophers, ancient and modern, have advocated suicide. Pagan communities, ancient and modern, have regularly placed babies out of doors to die. The Romans enjoyed watching gladiators kill each other and seeing Christians chewed up by lions. Widows in India were traditionally burned on their husbands' funeral pyres. Other twentieth-century pagans besides the Nazis, notably in black Africa and Cambodia, have practised genocide. Current arguments for abortion on demand and euthanasia by agreement show that some among us have already gone back to paganism at this point, and there is really no reason to expect that life will continue to be held sacred when the Bible is no longer revered. Pragmatic arguments for quietly killing those who can make no useful contribution to society, as the Nazis quietly killed off mental defectives, are at times obvious and appealing, and only Scripture has ever given any communities anywhere motives for protecting the weak and helpless. Take away Scripture, and there is no telling where neo-pagan pragmatism will stop.

Today's drift from the authority of Christian truth – indeed from acknowledging any external authority at all – is producing disintegrated and distracted individuals and a disordered and anarchic society. And it will continue to do so, with domestic, political and economic consequences that can hardly be happy. Can the decline be arrested? Unfortunately, great numbers in our churches have so lost touch with the Christian authority-principle that even when they see which way things are going (which they often do not), they can do nothing to stop the rot. Whether the forces of biblical faithfulness can reverse the steady secularizing of the West is something only time will show. The sole certainty is that apart from biblical faithfulness such a reversal is not possible. A church in which scriptural teaching is no longer authoritative is already going with the world and has no ground on which to stand against it. If today's trend cannot be reversed, then the outlook for tomorrow's world is bleak indeed.

Such is the position regarding authority. Now we must discuss freedom.

What is freedom?

Freedom, as was said, has become a word to conjure with. It is modern man's way to treat freedom as the supreme value in life. Everyone wants more freedom than he has, and the quick way to get a following is to lay claim to a formula whereby freedom may be increased. It makes Westerners feel good to see themselves as the 'free world', just as it must have made the late Bertrand Russell feel good to announce his anti-Christianity in an essay entitled 'A Free Man's Worship'. Politicians, lawyers, educationists and social planners, if asked in public what they are after, will certainly reply in terms of maximizing personal freedom. Many hail today's permissiveness as a social virtue because it gives freedom for deviant behaviour which less tolerant ages would not have countenanced. 'Liberty–equality–fraternity' was the war-cry of the French Revolution, and the testimony of liberation-movements, literature, pop songs and political rhetoric all over the world is that liberty is no less vehemently sought today than it was in eighteenth-century France.

But what *is* liberty? Under what circumstances are we genuinely free? Ask this question, and the solid-looking front of freedom-seekers breaks up at once. There is no agreement on the answer.

Basically there are two ways of conceiving freedom, and we have pointed to the first already. It is to view freedom as secular, external and this-worldly. It is essentially a matter of breaking bonds and abolishing restrictions and hardships. It seeks freedom *from* or freedom *not to*. Those who think thus of freedom have different ways of pursuing it. Some hit out. These are the revolutionaries, social, political and aesthetic, who constantly strive to overthrow 'the system'. Others drop out. These are the hippies, the counter-culturalists, those who hole

23

up in rural communes and farms, do their own thing and never mind what the rest of the world is doing. Still others throw out. In the name of humanism these jettison Christianity with its supposedly dehumanizing restraints on conduct. Such also are those who seek women's liberation by decrying the leadership role of men. The idea common to all these endeavours is that you gain freedom by negating something else.

The results are unimpressive. Revolutions turn out to be an exchange of one tyranny for another. Hippy-ness is found to be no passport to happiness. The self-styled 'freethinker' spends his strength denying what his parents or some other authority-figure once tried to teach him, and he never gets beyond it. Women denouncing male leadership end up mannish and loud. Is any of this recognizable as the freedom for which we all inwardly long? The idea that freedom is what you have when you have thrown off all that represses or constrains you is a false trail which leads nowhere save to puzzlement and disillusioned bitterness.

The second approach to freedom is distinctively Christian. It is evangelical, personal and positive. It defines freedom persuasively, that is, in terms which (so it urges) all should recognize as expressing what they are really after. These terms relate not to externals, which vary from age to age and person to person, but to the unchanging realities of the inner life. This definition starts with freedom *from* and freedom *not to* – in this case, freedom from the guilt and power of sin, and freedom not to be dominated by tyrannical self-will – but it centres on freedom *for*: freedom for God and godliness, freedom to love and serve one's Maker and fellow-creatures, freedom for the joy, hope and contentment which God gives to sinners who believe in Christ. The essence of freedom (so the claim runs) lies in these inward qualities of heart, of which modern secular man knows nothing.

This approach sees freedom as the inner state of all who are fulfilling the potential of their own created nature by worshipping and serving their Saviour-God from the heart. Their freedom is freedom not to do wrong, but to do right; not to break the moral law, but to keep it; not to forget God, but to cleave to him every moment, in every endeavour and relationship; not to abuse and exploit others, but to lay down one's life for them (*cf.* Jn. 15:12f.; 1 Jn. 3:16). Freedom for such free service and self-giving is beyond the capacity, even the comprehension, of fallen human nature. At first sight few can recognize it as freedom at all. Though it is really the way of life for which we were made, it so negates the self-absorbed lifestyle which we all instinctively choose that it seems to us anti-human and frightens us off. In fact, the only way anyone comes to know it at all is as the gift of the risen Christ, who affirms his penitent disciples in their self-denial and imparts his life to us as we give away our own.

One aspect of this freedom is *integrity*, that simplicity and purity of heart which, as Kierkegaard analysed it, consists in willing one thing, namely the will and glory of God, so that one's motives are freed from the taint of self-regard. A second aspect is *spontaneity*. Unlike the rule-ridden Pharisees, whom Jesus pictured living (as it were) by numbers, the free person in Christ invests creative enterprise and resourcefulness in the task of pleasing and praising God and doing good to one's fellows. Where the Pharisee's concern is to avoid doing wrong, the free person seeks to make the most and best of every situation, so that he is lively and sometimes breath-taking company. A final aspect is *contentment*, the fruit of God's gift of a joy within that increases all life's pleasures, stays with us whatever is present or lacking in our outward circumstances, and enables us to accept without bitterness the most acute forms of suffering and pain. In short, the free person is free for holiness, humanness and happiness – a freedom which surely merits its name.

Where does this freedom come from? Jesus Christ, the one perfectly free man that history has seen, is its source as well as its model. He himself said, 'If the Son sets you free, you will be free indeed' (Jn. 8:36; for biblical development of the thought see Rom. 6:1 – 7:6 and Gal. 4:21 – 6:10). The exchange from which this promise comes is worth noting. Jesus has said: 'If you hold to my teaching…the truth will set you free.' His Jewish hearers, bridling, had protested (with pathetic unrealism, in view of the Roman occupation), 'We…have never been slaves of anyone.' Their protest showed them to be thinking of freedom in the purely external terms whose inadequacy we noted. But Jesus replied that he was talking of real freedom, freedom by comparison with which mere external non-servitude is not freedom at all. The real freedom is freedom from sin, which brings with it sonship to God and eternal security. Jesus tells them that only those whom he himself has freed, as they have entrusted themselves to him, are free in this full sense.

Jesus did not say, nor do I, that freedom from external pressures is not worth seeking or should not actually be sought by those for whom true freedom has become a reality. That is a different issue. My point, rather, is that while enjoyment of external freedom does not guarantee a free heart, the freedom that Christ gives can be enjoyed – praise God! – whatever external pressures there may be.

Freedom, authority, Scripture

It must be plain that the second view of freedom is the profounder of the two, and since this freedom is bound up with personal salvation, social usefulness and the praise of God together, we should want to see everyone's feet set on the road to it. But that road takes the form of accepting authority – the authority of God the Creator, who designed and sustains our human nature and alone can tell us what best to do with it; the authority of Jesus Christ, God incarnate, the risen, reigning Son of God to whom all authority is given, who frees and keeps free those who continue in his word; the authority of Holy Scripture, which, as we shall see, is not just a witness to Christ's universal reign but is actually the instrument of it so far as men are concerned; and the authority of the Holy Spirit, who so opens and applies Scripture to our hearts that we discern Christ's will and are enabled to do it.

27

We saw earlier that accepting some external authority-principle is the precondition of order, integration and stable purpose in one's life. What I am saying now is that the only authority-principle which imparts these blessings in a way that brings final satisfaction and salvation is the personal divine authority of 'the man Christ Jesus' (1 Tim. 2:5), mediated by the Holy Spirit in and through the Bible. An ancient prayer addresses God as the one 'whom to serve is to be free' ('whose service is perfect freedom', as the Anglican Prayer Book renders it). That is the truth we must face. We cannot have the freedom we want until we receive it on God's terms, that is, by giving up our rebellious independence and letting God be God to us. Real freedom is only ever found under authority – God's authority in Christ, authority which reaches us via God's written Word.

Once our society knew this well, but for a century now the Bible has been so much in eclipse, even in the churches, that the formula may well strike some as novel and others as incredible, because of the high view of Scripture which it implies. So far from being novel, however, that high view is authentic Christianity, and so far from being incredible it has as strong a claim on our acceptance as has any Christian truth. To show this is my next task.

2

AUTHORITY
AND SCRIPTURE

Built into Christianity is a principle of authority. This is because Christianity is revealed religion. It claims that God has acted to make known his mind and will, and therefore his revelation has authority for our lives. Biblical religion is marked by certainty about beliefs and duties. The diffidence and indefiniteness of conviction which thinks of itself as becoming humility has no place or warrant in Scripture, where humility begins with taking God's word about things. All through the Bible God's servants appear as folk who know what God has told them and are living by that knowledge. This is true of patriarchs, prophets, psalmists, apostles, other lesser lights and supremely of the Lord Jesus Christ himself.

Certainty and authority

Focus on Christ for a moment. He was the Son of God incarnate and as such had no will of his own. It was his nature, as well as his duty and delight, to do his Father's will in everything. He is on record as having said, 'I do nothing on my own but speak just what the Father has taught me...I always do what pleases him' (Jn. 8:28f.; *cf.* 4:34; 5:30; 6:38; 8:26; 12:49f.; 14:31; 17:4). Jesus knew that his authority as his Father's Messianic agent depended on his remaining subject to the Father in this way (he commended the Roman centurion for seeing that, Mt. 8:10ff.).

That he was in his Father's will was to him a source of tremendous strength, as became very plain in the last week of his earthly life. One day he rode into Jerusalem at the head of a cheering crowd, like a king coming to be crowned. The next day, alone, he went through the temple like a hurricane, wrecking the bazaar in the Court of Gentiles, kicking out the stallholders, upsetting the bankers' desks and dazzling on-lookers by the fury with which he denounced the business routines he had thus disrupted. The authorities huddled. Two big demonstrations in two days! What for? And what next? The day after, 'while Jesus was walking in the temple courts, the chief priests, the teachers of the law and the elders came to him. "By what authority are you doing these things?" they asked' (Mk. 11:27, 28). Jesus replied that his authority, like John's baptism, was from God. He was doing his Father's will and knew it, as he showed again two days later in Gethsemane ('not as I will, but as you will...your will be done...it must happen in this way', Mt. 26:39, 42, 54). His Father's will was the constant mark of his life.

Jesus was divine. We are not. So it might be expected that Jesus' followers would be less certain about the Father's mind and will than he was. In the New Testament, however, it is not so, whatever may be true of some Christians today. 'Know' is a New Testament keyword, 'we know' a New Testament refrain. These writers claim that Christians know God, his work, his will and his ways, because they have received revelation from him. They tell us that God's self-revelation has taken the form not only of action but also of instruction. God, so they say, has spoken in and through what Jesus said (Heb. 1:1f. with 2:3). He has made known to apostles and prophets the secret of his eternal plan (Eph. 1:9f.; 3:3–11; *cf.* Rom. 16:25f.; 1 Cor. 2:6–11). Apostolic preachers relay his message 'not in words taught…by human wisdom but in words taught by the Spirit' (1 Cor. 2:13). We receive this as 'sound doctrine' (2 Tim. 4:3; Tit. 1:9; 2:1), 'the truth' (2 Thes. 2:10, 12, 13, *etc.*), 'the word of God' (1 Thes. 2:13, *etc.*) and thus gain sure and certain knowledge of God's mind. Modern theology will oppose the authority of Christ to that of Scripture, but in the New Testament bowing to Christ's Lordship and believing God-taught doctrine entail each other.

Believing and obedience

And believing must lead to obedience. Christians have constantly been in trouble for defying human authorities and challenging consensuses. Peter would not stop evangelizing when told to (Acts 4:19f.; 5:27ff.) and was in and out of prison as a result. Christians risked persecution in the early days by refusing the formalities of Roman state religion, just as latter-day African Christians have courted martyrdom by rejecting tribal rites. Athanasius sentenced himself to exile by standing against the Arian world. Luther jeopardized his life by refusing to recant at Worms. Christians today make themselves unpopular by opposing such social realities as the pornography trade and such social conveniences as abortion on demand. These are samples of the costly nonconformity which Christians have practised down the ages.

Why do they behave so awkwardly? Because, standing under God's authority, they are sure that his revelation requires them to act as they do at whatever personal cost. Luther said at Worms, 'My conscience is captive to the Word of God; to go against conscience is neither right nor safe; here I stand, there is nothing else I can do; God help me; amen.' The privilege of knowing God's truth with certainty and precision carries with it the responsibility of obeying that truth with equal precision. Christianity is no armchair faith, but a call to action.

The problem of authority

But here a difficulty arises: whose version of revealed truth should be accepted? Imagine the perplexity of the Galatian Christians the day they first had read to them the blistering sentences in which Paul goes after some who 'are trying to pervert the gospel of Christ' (Gal. 1:7). 'As for those agitators, I wish they would go the whole way and emasculate themselves!' (Gal. 5:12). Imagine too how the Colossian Christians must have gulped when they first heard the words of Paul (whom they had never met) cutting down the teacher who was delighting in 'false humility and the worship of angels' and who was puffed up 'with idle notions' (Col. 2:18). In each case Paul was squelching respected men whose teaching on faith and duty had hitherto been treated as true. Whom should believers then follow? Paul? Or their local pundits?

This problem is still with us. Roman Catholics, for example, say that Christians should treat the Pope as chief pastor of all Christendom and that his *ex cathedra* pronouncements, with those of councils, are infallible. They say that Christians should pray to Mary and see the eucharist as in some sense the church's sacrifice for its sins. With this Protestants disagree. Radicals deny Jesus' personal deity, objective sin-bearing, bodily resurrection and personal return. With this both Protestants and Catholics disagree. What should the plain Christian do when he finds his fellow-believers at odds about the truth and will of God, some telling him one thing, some another? What procedure should he follow in order to determine his own belief and behaviour?

1. *The church as authority*
The Christian may treat the consensus of the church as decisive, making ecclesiastical tradition and conviction his authoritative guide to the authoritative will of God. This is what the Roman Catholic and Eastern Orthodox churches, with some Anglicans, tell us we should do. The implications of this rule of procedure will vary for individuals according to what they mean by 'church' (church of Rome, early church, their own denomination or whatever), but the principle is clear. You should approach the

33

Bible as a product of the church and identify main-stream church teaching with the biblical faith. You should study Scripture by the light of that teaching and make Scripture fit in with it. Where the church has not pronounced, you may freely speculate. But you should take as from God all the definite teaching it gives. What the church says, God says. Therefore, the Holy Spirit's first step in teaching us is to make us docile under church authority.

2. *The individual as authority*
The Christian may treat his own ideas as decisive, whatever dissent from the Bible and the historic church that may involve. On this view, Scripture and church teaching are essentially resource material to help us make up our own minds. Both should be known. But neither need be endorsed, for neither is infallible and both include chaff as well as wheat. The theologies found in Scripture and Christian history are uneven attempts to verbalize a religious awareness in such terms as different cultures provided, and each is a mixture of facts and fancies, insights and mistakes. Our task is to sort out what seems lastingly valid and express that in today's terms. The principle is that what our own spirit says – that is, our reason, conscience and imagination – God says. The Spirit's work is to sensitize our spirit to discern God's message to us in this way.

3. *The Bible as authority*
The Christian may treat Holy Scripture as decisive, according to the dictum of the Westminster Confession: 'The supreme judge by which all controver-

sies of religion are to be determined, and all decrees of councils, opinions of ancient writers, doctrines of men, and private spirits, are to be examined, and in whose sentence we are to rest, can be no other but the Holy Spirit speaking in the Scripture' (I, x). One who takes this line departs from the second view by receiving the Bible as God's authoritative instruction for all time, and from the first view by subjecting the church's teaching and interpretations to the judgment of the Bible itself as a self-interpreting whole. He will look to the Holy Spirit who gave Scripture to authenticate its contents to God's people as God's truth, and to show them how it applies to their lives (*cf.* 1 Jn. 2:20-27). His constant aim will be to have Scripture judge and correct all human ideas, including his own. He will value the church's doctrinal and expository heritage but not give it the last word. His heart echoes Augustine's breathtaking words to God: 'What your Scripture says, you say.' He views the Spirit's teaching role as one first and foremost of keeping minds attuned to Scripture, the divine textbook.

To illustrate how these alternatives might work, let us imagine a debate about abortion on demand. An adherent of the first approach (call him a *traditionalist* or an *ecclesiasticist*) would oppose the practice because the church has always forbidden it. An adherent of the third approach (call him a *biblicist* or an *evangelical*) would oppose the practice because Scripture forbids killing people and will not let us see the foetus as anything less than a person heading for a viable life. The adherent of the second approach

35

(call him a *subjectivist* or a *relativist*) might well dismiss the biblical view of the foetus as unscientific, and prohibitions based on it as groundless and inappropriate, and might defend abortion on demand as compassionate to women, urging that unwanted babies are a bad thing and that modern medical technology makes the operation pretty safe.

Between these alternative methods of determining God's will you and I must choose. They are not compatible, even when on particular points all three yield coinciding convictions. The first and the third, which both view Scripture as revealed truth that abides, are closer to each other than either is to the second, which treats biblical thought as a transient cultural product. Yet the gap between these two is wide, as the historic tension between Roman Catholicism and evangelical Protestantism shows. Individuals may and do oscillate inconsistently between the three alternatives, but each in itself excludes the two others.

Which method, then, is right? Which is authentically. Christian? Which squares with the teaching and purpose of Christ and his apostles? Which would Jesus and Paul and John and Peter approve, were they back with us today to guide us? I think the answer is plain.

Christ's view of authority

Take Jesus first. There is no good reason to doubt the authenticity of what the Gospels say of him. They were evidently written in good faith and with great care by knowledgeable persons (*cf.* Lk. 1:1–4; Jn. 19:35; 21:24). They were composed at a time when Jesus was still remembered and misstatements about him could be nailed. They were accepted everywhere, it seems, as soon as they were known, though the early Christians were not credulous and detected spurious gospels with skill. The consensus of the centuries has been that these four portraits of Jesus have a ring of truth. While it is easy to believe that so awesome and unconventional a figure as Jesus, with his divine self-awareness and claims, would be well remembered — would, indeed, prove unforgettable — it is not credible that he could have been made up. It is safe to say that not even Shakespeare, who created Lear, Hamlet and Falstaff, could have invented Jesus Christ! Granted, individual scholars doubt gospel facts and details, but in every field of study there is always some scholar ready to query what his peers affirm, and anyone who reflects on the probabilities of the case will soon see that such paradoxical doubts should not weigh heavily with straightforward people. We may be confident that in reading the Gospels we meet the real Jesus. From them we learn the following facts.

1. *Jesus' authority*

Jesus claimed absolute personal authority in all his teaching: 'It was said...but I tell you' (Mt. 5:21ff.); 'He taught as one who had authority, and not as their teachers of the law' (Mt. 7:29); 'Heaven and earth will pass away, but my words will never pass away' (Mk. 13:31). He said that our destiny depends on whether, having heard his words, we heed them or not (Mt. 7:24–27; Lk. 6:47–49); 'There is a judge for the one who rejects me and does not accept my words; that very word which I spoke will condemn him at the last day. For I did not speak of my own accord, but the Father who sent me commanded me what to say and how to say it...So whatever I say is just what the Father has told me to say' (Jn. 12:48–50).

2. *Old Testament authority*

Jesus taught the absolute divine authority of the Jewish Scriptures. Some 200 references in the Gospels combine to make his view of our Old Testament crystal clear. He saw the books as having both human authors and a divine author, so that, for example, commands which Moses presents as the word of God are indeed such (Mk. 7:8–13) and an expository comment in Genesis 2:24 can be quoted as what 'the Creator...said' (Mt. 19:5). As God's word, disclosing his truth, purpose and command, Scripture has abiding authority (Jn. 10:35; Mt. 5:18–20).

It is striking to see how Jesus, while setting his personal authority against that of earlier rabbinic interpreters (which is what he was doing when he contrasted what 'was said' with what 'I tell you'), always bowed and taught others to bow to Scripture as such. He gave the key to his whole ministry when he said, 'Do not think that I have come to abolish the Law or the Prophets; I have not come to abolish them but to fulfil them' (Mt. 5:17), that is, to be fully subject to them as they applied to him. From Scripture he resolved questions of doctrine (the resurrection, Mk. 12:24–27; the intended perma-

nence of marriage, Mt. 19:5f.) and ethics (the right-
ness of letting need override sabbath restrictions,
Mt. 12:2–8; the wrongness of *corban* casuistry as a
cop-out from the obligations of the fifth command-
ment, Mk. 7:10–13). By Scripture he justified the
acts of his ministry (cleansing the temple,
Mk. 11:15–17). By it he discerned his personal
calling to be the Servant-Messiah who must enter
into his reign by the path of death and resurrection
(Mt. 26:53–56; Mk. 12:10f., 14:21; Lk. 18:31ff.;
22:37; 24:25ff.; 44ff.; *cf.* Mt. 4:4, 7, 10). His resurrection was his vindication, the Father's seal of approval
set publicly on all the Son had said and done –
including what he said about Scripture and his
going to Jerusalem to die in obedience to Scripture.
It is surely significant that on the resurrection day
he was found with two groups of disciples explaining
how Scripture had been fulfilled in his dying and
rising to reign (Lk. 24:25ff., 46ff.).

3. *New Testament authority*
Jesus conferred his own authority on the apostles to
go out in his name as his witnesses and spokesmen.
In appointing them his messengers, Jesus promised
them the Spirit to enable them to fulfil their task
(Mk. 13:11; Lk. 24:47ff.; Jn. 14:25f.; 15:26f.; 16:7–15,
20:21–23; Acts 1:8), and he prayed for his people,
present and future, in just two categories; first, the
apostles; second, 'those who will believe in me
through their message' (Jn. 17:20). Thus, he showed
that the apostles' witness would be both the norm
and the means of all other Christians' faith to the
end of time.

Apostolic authority

The rest of the New Testament is as we would expect in light of these facts. On the one hand, the apostles are conscious of their role as Christ's commissioned representatives and of the God-givenness and divine authority of their teaching. This is especially clear in Paul and John, who both addressed situations where their authority had been challenged. In 1 Corinthians 2:12f. Paul claims both inward illumination and verbal inspiration for his message. In 1 Corinthians 14:37f. and 2 Thessalonians 3:6–12 he insists that his directives must be taken as commands of the Lord whom he represents. In Galatians 1:8f. he solemnly curses anyone who brings a different message from his own.

John calmly but breathtakingly states in black and white that 'We [apostolic witnesses] are from God, and whoever knows God listens to us; but whoever is not from God does not listen to us. This is how we recognize the Spirit of truth and the spirit of falsehood' (1 Jn 4:6). Bolder authority-claims could hardly be made. The apostles are no less sure than were the Old Testament prophets that their message was from God.

But, on the other hand, with equal emphasis they claim the Jewish Scriptures as divine instructions for Christians, prophetically proclaiming Christ, the gospel and the realities of discipleship to the church. 'The holy Scriptures...are able to make you wise for salvation through faith in Christ Jesus. All Scripture is God-breathed and is useful for teaching, rebuking, correcting and training in righteousness, so that the man of God may be thoroughly equipped for every good work' (2 Tim. 3:15-17). Of what he calls 'the prophetic writings' or 'the oracles of God' Paul declares, 'Everything that was written in the past was written to teach us, so that through endurance and the encouragement of the Scriptures we [Christians] might have hope' (Rom. 15:4; *cf.* 1 Cor. 10:11). Old Testament passages are quoted as God's speech in Acts (4:25; 28:25) and Hebrews (3:7; 10:15), and Paul's phrases 'the Scripture says to Pharaoh' (Rom. 9:17) and 'the Scripture foresaw...and announced the gospel in advance to Abraham' (Gal. 3:8) show how completely he himself equated Scripture with God speaking – we might even say, God preaching. That the Jewish Scriptures have God's plan concerning Christ as their main subject is everywhere taken for granted. In Hebrews, the deity, manhood and mediation of Christ are the doctrinal themes, and every point up to the start of chapter 13 is made by expounding and applying the Old Testament. The New Testament view of the Old is consistent and clear.

So the Jewish Scriptures were held to be authoritative God-given witness to Christ, just as apostolic preaching was. In both cases the authority was seen not as human, the relative yet uneven authority of insight and expertise, but as divine, the absolute, oracular authority of God telling truth about his work and his will, and about the worship and obedience that we owe him. Not all that was said whether by the Old Testament or by the apostles was equally important, but all was part of the rule of faith and life since it came from God.

Since Jewish Scripture and apostolic preaching were on a par, it was as natural as it was momentous that Peter, having reminded his readers that Old Testament writings came as 'men...were carried along by the Holy Spirit' (2 Pet. 1:21), should bracket Paul's sermons on paper (which is what his letters were) with 'the other Scriptures' (3:16) and admonish his readers to heed both and not mishandle either. Here the Christian authority principle at last becomes explicit: the Old Testament read in conjunction with the apostolic presentation of Christ or, putting it the other way round, the apostolic presentation of Christ conjoined with the Old Testament is the rule of faith for Jesus' disciples. God now teaches, reproves, corrects and instructs in and by what is written in the two Testaments together.

Despite the newness of the New Testament, the principle that the written Word of God must shape faith and life was old. The basis of Old Testament religion was that God has spoken in human language and has caused his teaching to be recorded for permanence, and that the way to please him is to go by the book. All Jesus' teaching and ministry assumed this. What follows, then? Should we say that he founded Christianity on a fallacy? Or should we not rather say that by endorsing this basic Jewish tenet he showed that it was true?

Here we reach a crucial point for our own faith. So far we have been appealing to the Bible simply as a good historical source, from which we may learn with certainty what the founders of Christianity taught. But if Jesus was God incarnate and spoke with personal divine authority, and if by sending the Spirit he really enabled his apostles to speak God's word with total consistency, it follows that both Testaments (that which his gift of the Spirit produced as well as that which he knew and authenticated) ought to be received as 'the very words of God' and as 'God-breathed and...useful...so that the man of God may be thoroughly equipped' (Rom. 3:2; 2 Tim. 3:16, 17). Only as we seek to believe and do what the two Testaments, taken together, say, have we the full right to call ourselves Jesus' disciples. 'Why do you call me, "Lord, Lord," and do not do what I say?' (Lk. 6:46). Scripture comes to us, as it were, from Jesus' hand, and its authority and his are so interlocked as to be one.

Bowing to the living Lord entails submitting mind and heart to the written Word. Disciples individually and churches corporately stand under the authority of Scripture because they stand under the Lordship of Christ, who rules by Scripture. This is not bibliolatry but Christianity in its most authentic form.

Biblical authority
So we learn from Christ to learn from Scripture as God's authoritative Word. We may spell out the theology of that lesson as follows.

1. *The Creator communicates*
God made us in his image, rational and responsive, so that he and we might live in fellowship. To this end, he makes himself known to us. He enters into communication with a view to communion. Always

he has caused his works of creation and providence to mediate some sense of his reality, righteousness and glory to all who are alive in this world, however little they welcome this. 'Since the creation of the world God's invisible qualities – his eternal power and divine nature – have been clearly seen, being understood from what has been made' (Rom. 1:20; *cf*. 1:32; 2:14ff.; Acts 14:16f.; Ps. 19:1ff.). Moreover, God speaks in words, using his own gift of language to tell us about himself. We read that verbal revelation began in Eden before man fell (Gn. 2:16f.) and that all that God has made known for salvation was revealed verbally to and through patriarchs, prophets, apostles and Jesus Christ, after which it was embodied in the Bible (Rom. 15:4; Gal. 3:8; Eph. 3:4ff.; Heb. 2:3; 1 Pet. 1:10ff.).

2. *God reveals salvation*
The general formula is that God reveals himself so that we may know him. The specific formula is that God reveals himself as Saviour so that sinners may know him savingly. Here are four connected strands of divine activity.

First and most basic was God's historical self-disclosure by redemptive deeds prefaced and followed by explanatory words, a sequence of acts that began with the patriarchs and the exodus and reached its climax in the Messianic ministry, atoning death and triumphant resurrection of Jesus, whereby, as Zechariah sang, God 'raised up a horn of salvation for us in the house of his servant David' (Lk. 1:69). The good news of these acts is the *gospel*.

Second and distinct from this was God's work of

inspiring expository, celebratory and applicatory records of his words and deeds, so that all might know what he had done and would do, and what their response should be. The collection of these records is the *Bible*.

The third strand in God's revelatory work is his providential action in bringing to each individual's notice what Holy Scripture has made public and permanently available. He does this through his messengers who spread the good news. The generic name for this activity, which includes all forms of instruction and is meant to involve all God's people, is *preaching*.

Fourth and following on from the third is the giving of understanding so that those instructed believe the message and commit themselves to the Saviour who is its subject. This inner enlightening is called revelation in Matthew 11:27; 16:17 and Galatians 1:16, but the usual name for it is *illumination*, according to the imagery of 2 Corinthians 4:6 and Ephesians 1:17–21.

All four modes of divine action – redemptive revelation in history, didactic revelation in Scripture, relayed revelation in the church's preaching and teaching, and illuminative revelation in the hearer's heart – are necessary if we are to know God as Saviour through Christ. The first two modes ceased in the first century AD, but the third and fourth continue. The fourth is necessary because, although the Bible message authenticates itself as God's truth by the light and power that flow from it, fallen men are unresponsive and indeed resistant to it, so that without illumination the gospel will only

45

be doubted, devalued and finally ignored (Lk. 14: 15–24; 2 Cor. 4:3ff.). God must enable us to see what he has revealed to the world in Jesus Christ, or we shall stay blind to it.

3. *God's Spirit teaches through Scripture*
The Spirit of Christ who indwells Christians never leads them to doubt, criticize, go beyond or fall short of Bible teaching. Spirits which do that are not the Spirit of Christ (1 Jn. 4:1–6). Rather, the Spirit makes us appreciate the divine authority of Scripture, so that we accept its account of spiritual realities and live as it calls us to do. As the Spirit gave the Word by brooding over its human writers and leading the church to recognize their books as its canon for belief and behaviour, so now he becomes the authoritative interpreter of Scripture as he shows us how biblical teaching bears on our living.

To be sure, what Bible books meant as messages to their first readers can be gleaned from commentaries. But what they mean for our lives today is something we learn only as the Spirit stirs our insensitive consciences. Never does the Spirit draw us away from the written Word, any more than from the living Word. Instead, he keeps us in constant, conscious, contented submission to both together. He exerts his authority precisely by making real to us the authority of Christ and of Scripture – more precisely, the authority of Christ *through* Scripture. This is what it means to be Spirit-led.

4. *Scripture promotes ethics*

Some fear that full acceptance of biblical authority must result in a legalistic lifestyle. The root of their fear seems to be a belief that God's law in Scripture really is a code of mechanical, impersonal do's and don'ts, in other words, that the Pharisees' view of the law was essentially right. But Jesus' scorching comments on the Pharisees showed that this view is wrong. The truth is that the moral teaching of Scripture focuses the ideal of creative goodness which Christ actually lived out. It requires us not just to stay within the limits of specific commands and prohibitions but to stay within those limits so that we can make the best of every situation and relationship for the glory of God and the good of others. Law-keeping must be love in action. This is the one truth embedded in the otherwise false scheme of 'situation ethics', which refuses to accept the law laid down in Scripture as the teaching of God. The ethical creativity which is always asking what is the best we can do is one dimension of that Christlike holiness to which we are called, and those who believe most strongly in the authority of Scripture should be manifesting more of this quality than anyone else.

5. *Scripture controls Christian consciences*

Consciences not governed by God's Word are to that extent not Christian. 'God alone is Lord of the conscience, and hath left it free from the doctrines and commandments of men, which are, in any thing, contrary to His Word' says the Westminster Confession (XX, ii). One thinks again of Luther's state-

47

ment at Worms: 'My conscience is captive to the Word of God: to go against conscience is neither right nor safe.' If conforming to ecclesiastical, governmental, marital or parental demands involves action contrary to Scripture, God can be served only by non-conformity at that point. This may put us out of step with others and prove costly to us, but nothing less will please God. Conversely, when we find Scripture requiring of us goals and standards which are not the way of the world (going the second mile, turning the other cheek, loving our enemies) we may not excuse ourselves by reflecting that nobody else behaves like that. 'Do not conform any longer to the pattern of this world,' wrote Paul, 'but be transformed by the renewing of your mind. Then you will be able to test and approve what God's will is – his good, pleasing and perfect will' (Rom. 12:2). 'Test and approve' is one Greek word, signifying the discernment of a consecrated conscience applying the generalities of God's Word to the specifics of one's personal life.

Scripture and freedom
We saw earlier that true freedom is only ever found under God's authority. What we are seeing now is that it is only ever found under the authority of Scripture, through which God's authority is mediated to men and Christ by his Spirit rules his people's lives. Biblical authority is often expounded in opposition to lax views of truth. Not so often, however, is it presented as the liberating, integrating, invigorating principle that it really is. The common idea is that unqualified confidence in the

Bible leads to narrow-minded inhibitions and crippling restraints on what you may think and do. The truth is that such confidence produces liberated living – living, that is, which is free from uncertainty, doubt and despair – which otherwise is not found anywhere. The person who trusts his Bible knows what God did, does and will do, what he commands and what he promises. With the Colossians, the Bible-believer understands 'God's grace in all its truth' (Col. 1:6), for the Christ of Scripture has become his Saviour, master and friend. Since Scripture shines as a lamp to his feet and a light to his path (Ps. 119:105), he can pick his way through the pitfalls of our spiritually benighted world without stumbling and travel through life with what the title of a famous old tract called 'safety, certainty and enjoyment'.

Such is the freedom (and the victory) found under the authority of the Bible. Such is the basic shape and style of the life in which the fullness of God's power comes to be known. And who can do without that? There are few aspects of the Christian message with which the church and the world need so urgently to be faced as the truth – the precious, stabilizing, enriching truth – of the full trustworthiness and divine authority of the written Word of God.

3

AUTHORITY
AND INERRANCY

Is our argument finished? Not quite. One matter
still calls for discussion.

The fashion in scholarship

I said at the start that in the realm of belief, authority
belongs to truth and truth only. I stick to that. I can
make no sense – no reverent sense, anyway – of the
idea, sometimes met, that God speaks his truth to
us in and through false statements by biblical
writers, any more than I can make moral sense of
Plato's commendation of the useful lie. Accordingly,
I have reasoned about the authority of Scripture on
the assumption that it contains God-taught truth
throughout.

But at this many sceptical eyebrows go up. For
the past hundred years among Protestants most
books published on the Bible, most teachers in most
seminaries and most clergy in most churches have
told the world that scientific study of the Scriptures
(called 'critical' because it consciously evaluates its
data) has made it impossible to believe all that the
Bible says. The cumulative effect of critical theories

about authorship, which view some books of both Testaments as spurious and so as spoofs; of critical theories about composition, which see historical matter in both Testaments as fanciful latter-day invention; and of critical claims that Scripture is chock-a-block with irreconcilable contradictions; has been to produce an atmosphere in which most folks seem convinced, on the say-so not just of unbelievers but of the Protestant academic establishment, that sensible persons must now treat the trustworthiness of the Bible as an exploded myth.

It should be added, to complete the picture, that whereas Roman Catholicism officially held to full biblical inerrancy till the second Vatican Council, its scholars have recently swallowed a great deal of Protestant scepticism so that it looks as if the older belief will soon be a minority position in Catholicism too.

How should this state of affairs be viewed? I offer the following comments.

First, we should recognize the ingenuity of critical theories and the ability of their exponents. To think of these latter, as some have done, as if they were cretins and crooks, lacking academic ability and integrity just as they lack some elements of Christian orthodoxy, is a mistake. They have in fact been people of rare distinction, and the current dominance of their viewpoint is testimony to the persuasive skill with which they have expounded it.

Second, we should understand that the critical approach is nowadays an accepted convention of professional biblical scholarship. Sociologists of knowledge distinguish between *theories* and *para-*

digms, defining the latter as the presuppositional frame of reference within which theories are formed. Whereas biblical infallibility was once a paradigm for Christian scholars in all fields, biblical fallibility is the accepted paradigm today.

I once heard a British university professor of theology tell a conference of his peers that New Testament studies are currently healthy, for everything held by anybody is being challenged by somebody. Modern academics, like ancient Athenians, enjoy having new theories to dissect, and it is understandable (if regrettable) that a biblical technician should treat a rank growth of critical opinions as a good sign. Then, too, many theologians today seem to feel that they owe it to their non-Christian peers in other disciplines to doubt as much as they can of their own Christianity and so escape the suspicion of being bigoted – a quixotic policy which seems as goofy as it does gratuitous. (Do Marxist academics behave like that?) But the fact remains that biblical scepticism is in fashion as a paradigm of scholarship. It is regarded as an academic virtue. Your scholarly credentials become suspect if you disclaim it, and many teachers make a point of pushing it down students' throats to deliver them from what is seen as naive credulity and the closed mind. Like other things taken for granted, it is not easily challenged. He who threatens a sacred cow finds great crowds threatening him and is made to feel very much the odd man out.

Third, we should note that biblical scepticism, even in small doses, has effects that reach further than career academics in their ivory towers sometimes see. In principle, it marks abandonment of the axiom that what Scripture says, God says. Once that happens – once, that is, you give up the New Testament view of biblical inspiration – there is no limit on how far you will go in rejecting or relativizing biblical assertions, save your own arbitrary will. Protestantism's current confusion is largely due to the way its teachers have fanned out at this point, producing as many different sub-biblical theologies as there have been thinkers to devise them.

Fourth, we should realize that this whole development of biblical study, however dazzling in detail, is unnecessary. Biblical criticism developed in Germany had scepticism built into it from the start in the form of Kant's denial that God communicates verbally with men (a denial which strikes at the Bible's main claim and message), plus the eighteenth-century rationalist assumption that miracles do not happen. Naturally, the scepticism present in its premises comes out in its conclusions. But today, as in the past, a responsible biblical scholarship exists with the full truth of Scripture as its basic premise. It keeps its end up convincingly (so I judge) when interacting with critical opinion. It copes with the phenomena of Scripture, including the apparent discrepancies, at least as plausibly as does scholarship of the sceptical kind. The works of reference and resource which it produces stand comparison with any written from a rival standpoint. (Look at the *Tyndale* and *New International* commentary series, *The New Bible Dictionary* and *The New International Dictionary of New Testament Theology* if you want to verify that.) While Bible-believing scholarship thus maintains itself, the claim that Holy Scripture can no longer be regarded as wholly trustworthy is plain nonsense.

Affirming inerrancy

A further point arises. It concerns the word *inerrancy*, which Protestants and Roman Catholics have been using for more than a century to denote the quality of entire trustworthiness which Bible-believers ascribe to the written Word. Those who hold themselves free to disbelieve details of what the Bible tells us naturally disclaim belief in inerrancy. James Barr, for instance, sees the linking of biblical authority with inerrancy as the essence of Fundamentalism, from which he shrinks with scorn. Others, however, who claim to cleave to all that Scripture teaches nonetheless object to the word and carefully avoid it when spelling out their faith in Scripture, as if they do not think it fits the facts. This is perplexing.

The fact seems to be that these folk run scared. They are frightened of certain mental attitudes and stances with which they feel the word *inerrancy* is now inseparably linked and which in their view tend to obscure the Bible's main message and make against the best in biblical scholarship. Specifically, they hear the inerrancy-claim as challenging all comers to find mistakes in Scripture if they can – which, so they think, is an improper diverting of interest from the great issues of the gospel to the minutiae of Bible harmony, and from believing proclamation to rationalistic apologetics. Also, they

55

hear the inerrancy-claim as implying that the whole Bible can be proved true by secular inquiry, and as centring attention on questions of its scientific and historical correctness. They think the claim leads to a sort of interpretation that overlooks the width of the cultural gap between Bible times and our own, and the extent to which our criteria of truth and accuracy fail to apply to biblical material. Because they wish to dissociate themselves from these tendencies, they decline to speak of inerrancy.

I sympathize. Yet I wonder if they have chosen the wisest and most fruitful course of action. I say this as one who over the years has moved in the opposite direction. Once I too avoided the word *inerrancy* as much as I could, partly because I had no wish myself to endorse the tendencies mentioned and partly because the word has a negative form and I like to sound positive. But I find that nowadays I need the word. Verbal currency, as we know, can be devalued. Any word may have some of its meaning rubbed off, and this has happened to all my preferred terms for stating my belief about the Bible. I hear folk declare Scripture *inspired* and in the next breath say that it misleads from time to time. I hear them call it *infallible* and *authoritative*, and find they mean only that its impact on us and the commitment to which it leads us will keep us in God's grace, not that it is all true.

This is not enough for me. I want to safeguard the historic evangelical meaning of these three words and to make clear my intention, as a disciple of Jesus Christ, to receive as from the Father and the Son all that Scripture, when properly interpreted, proves to be affirming. So I assert inerrancy after all. I think this is a clarifying thing to do, since it shows what I mean when I call Scripture inspired, infallible and authoritative. In an era of linguistic devaluation and double-talk we owe this kind of honesty to one another.

Let me not be misheard. I am not saying that I would rather speak of inerrancy than of infallibility, were I free to choose. In Britain (and I am, after all, British) *infallibility* is the older and more familiar term, which while it retains the clear strong sense it has always had in UCCF parlance is also more appropriate; for it points to the function of Scripture as guide and authority, whereas *inerrancy* indicates no more than its factual correctness. All I mean is that when the old words are used in reduced senses, it makes for clarity and straightforwardness to affirm inerrancy alongside infallibility, and to explain that the latter both entails and rests on the former.

So inerrancy must, I think, be affirmed by those who would come clean in their witness to the God of the Bible. Assertors of inerrancy, however, need constantly to be making two points if misunderstandings are to be avoided. The first is negative, the second positive.

First, the assertion of inerrancy *does not bear directly on the task of exegesis*. Exegesis means drawing from each passage the meaning and message which it was conveying to its writer's own first readers. The exegetical task is to read everything out of the text while taking care to read nothing into it. Biblical interpretation comprises exegesis, followed by a synthesis of findings within a biblical frame of reference, followed by application for the guidance of faith and life today. Moreover, it must be done throughout in a way that can be justified from biblical data and is free from prejudices imported from the thought-world of today's culture. Belief in inerrancy will affect the rigour with which one synthesizes and applies, but in exegesis the question is not yet one of truth, only one of meaning, and the assertion of inerrancy is not a shortcut to determining what texts mean. We can do that only by studying the flow of thought to which each text belongs. To be sure, when one of two grammatically possible meanings conflicts with what the same writer says elsewhere, the inerrantist will see this as weighing in favour of the other. This, however, is not theological bias, but the respect for one's author which serious students of any documents, biblical or otherwise, will show. Serious students will never needlessly accuse any author of muddle-headed self-contradiction. In this, inerrantists and non-inerrantists are on exactly the same footing.

Second, the assertion of inerrancy *bears directly on our theological method*. What it says is that in formulating my theology I shall not consciously deny, disregard or arbitrarily relativize anything that I find Bible writers teaching, nor cut the knot of any problem of Bible harmony, factual or theological, by assuming that the writers were not consistent with themselves or with each other. Instead, I shall try to harmonize and integrate all that is taught (without remainder), to take it as from God (however little I may like it), and to seek actively to live by it (whatever change of present beliefs and behaviour-patterns it may require). This is what acceptance of the Bible wholly God-given and totally true requires of us.

Freedom trail

In Boston, Massachusetts, there is an official Freedom Trail, a tour of key sites connected with the War of Independence. Christianity knows another freedom trail, which the foregoing pages have sought to point out. The Boston freedom trail celebrates the gaining of political independence through fighting the British. The Christian freedom trail has to do with surrendering personal independence as one ceases to fight God. The point I have sought to make is that the freedom for which we were created is only ever enjoyed under the authority of God in Christ, and the only way we come under that authority and stay under it is by submitting in faith and obedience to what is in the Bible. The path to true personal freedom under God is acknowledgment of the authority of the Bible and its Christ. The gospel finds us rebels, guilty, lost and hopeless, and leads us for salvation to the feet of Christ, who teaches us to live by Scripture.

The importance of recognizing biblical inerrancy as a fact of faith is that, on the one hand, it reminds us that all Scripture is instruction in one way or another from the God of truth, and, on the other, it commits us to consistency in believing, receiving and obeying everything that it proves to say. The more completely heart and mind are controlled by Scripture, the fuller our freedom and the greater our joy. God's free person knows God and knows about God. He observes God-taught standards and restraints in his living and in his relationships. He trusts God's promises, and in the power of Bible certainties lives out his days in peace and hope. Modern man needs to hear from the church more of this message of freedom. The church needs to learn again how basic to that message is the truth of the inerrancy of Scripture, on which the fullness of biblical authority depends.

We have reached a place in the history of our culture where stable relationships based on respect, goodwill, fidelity and service are breaking down and alienation is becoming commonplace. Husbands and wives, parents and children, students and their instructors, employers and their employees, are increasingly estranged from each other in loneliness and hostility. A new and nasty feature of this eroding of relationships is that it is justified in the name of freedom, meaning the abandoning of restrictions and restraints. Actually, the idea that freedom requires uncommittedness or an adversary relationship toward other people is a sign of how far our society has drifted from its former understanding of what it means to be truly human and (equally important) godly. Our negative attitudes in relationships and our insistence in doing our own thing, pursuing personal pleasure no matter who gets hurt, show that we are not really free at all. We are estranged not merely from people but also from God and are in bondage to the grim perversion of nature which the Bible calls sin.

'When you were slaves to sin', wrote Paul to the Roman Christians, 'you were free from the control of righteousness. What benefit did you reap at that time from the things you are now ashamed of? Those things result in death! But now that you have been set free from sin and have become slaves to God' (which is what becoming a Christian means; when you put your trust in Jesus Christ you become God's slave through repentance and are freed from sin's dominion by regeneration), 'the benefit you reap leads to holiness, and the result is eternal life. For the wages of sin is death, but the gift of God is eternal life in Christ Jesus our Lord' (Rom. 6:20ff.).

True freedom – freedom from sin, freedom for God and righteousness – is found where Jesus Christ is Lord in living personal fellowship. It is under the authority of a fully trusted Bible that Christ is most fully known and this God-given freedom most fully enjoyed. If therefore we have at heart spiritual renewal for society, for churches and for our own lives, we shall make much of the entire trust worthiness – that is, the inerrancy – of Holy Scripture as the inspired and liberating Word of God.

Also by J. I. Packer

GOD'S WORDS
Studies of key Bible themes

'This book', writes the author, 'takes keywords from the
Bible and spells out in a practical way some of the main
thoughts linked with them. The goal is understanding, faith
and wisdom.'

Dr Packer goes on to examine essential Bible words such as
sin, grace, fellowship, death, regeneration, holiness. Here is
Christian doctrine in crystal-clear language, warm, vigorous
and energizing.

Inter-Varsity Press   *Paper, 224pp.*